HQ NAVAL MATERIAL COMMAND INSTRUCTION   NAVMATINST 4790.26

HQ US ARMY MATERIEL DEVELOPMENT AND READINESS COMMAND REGULATION DARCOM-R 700-106

HQ AIR FORCE LOGISTICS COMMAND REGULATION   AFLCR 66-80

HQ AIR FORCE SYSTEMS COMMAND REGULATION   AFSCR 66-80

HQ US MARINE CORPS ORDER   MCO P4790.9

LOGISTICS

I0426065

DEPOT MAINTENANCE
PRODUCTION CAPACITY
MEASUREMENT AND REPORTING PROCEDURES

26 March 1982

DEPARTMENTS OF THE NAVY, THE ARMY, THE AIR FORCE AND THE MARINE CORPS

DEPARTMENTS OF THE NAVY, ARMY, AIR FORCE, AND MARINE CORPS

Headquarters Naval Material Command Crystal Plaza, Washington, DC 20360	NAVMATINST 4790.26
Headquarters Army Materiel Development and Readiness Command 5001 Eisenhower Ave., Alexandria, VA 22333	DARCOM REGULATION 700-106
Headquarters Air Force Logistics Command Wright-Patterson Air Force Base, OH 45433	AFLC REGULATION 66-80
Headquarters Air Force Systems Command Andrews Air Force Base, DC 20334	AFSC REGULATION 66-80
Headquarters US Marine Corps Washington, DC 20380	MCO P4790.9

26 March 1982

Logistics

DEPOT MAINTENANCE
PRODUCTION CAPACITY
MEASUREMENT AND REPORTING PROCEDURES

Recommended changes may be submitted by affected service activities as need arises. All recommendations for additions, deletions, and corrections, including individual service supplements regarding implementation of the procedures and functional processes stated herein or in the cited directives will be processed through the Service headquarters to JADMAG for resolution prior to implementation. Recommendations or comments will be identified to the specific page, paragraph, and line in the text. The proposed version should be submitted with sufficient rationale to support the recommended change.

Purpose: This publication provides the procedures which the logistics elements of the military services have established to accomplish the intent of DOD 4151.15H, and DOD 7220.29H as they apply to Depot Maintenance Production Capacity determination. These procedures provide uniform implementing guidance with the express intent to facilitate realistic and consistent physical capacity measurement and reporting which will be uniform shop by shop throughout every military facility performing depot maintenance workload. Physical capacity, as collected under these procedures, will be used as a baseline for determining both peacetime and war mobilization posture.

OPR: NMC/MAT-04J
     DARCOM
     AFLC/MAX
     AFSC/SDD
     USMC

DISTRIBUTION: (See Page 42)

i

TABLE OF CONTENTS

Chapter 1

INTRODUCTION

1-1 Background

The Joint Logistics Commanders (JLC) chartered the Joint Aeronautical Depot Maintenance Action Group (JADMAG) to develop and recommend, for JLC approval and implementation, policy and actions necessary to assure effective and efficient aeronautical depot maintenance in support of service missions.

A specific task assignment of JADMAG to accomplish its mission is to obtain uniform capacity measurement and reporting by each depot. Consistency and accuracy among the services are required in the application of DOD 4151.15H to determine both physical and peacetime capacities. Stated capacities have significant impact on the accommodation of depot level workloads associated with the mobilization/combat support base.

The collection of capacity data must be in specific formats and at reporting levels compatible with collection of workload and other data. Compatibility is essential for application of analysis techniques by JADMAG. Coordination with service logistics staffs is necessary to accomplish this tasking. Development of these procedures was in concert with the service staffs whose influence provided for the future inclusion of non-aeronautical commodity groups. Each service will implement the uniform capacity measurement guidance contained here with JADMAG providing an overall coordinating and monitoring effort for the aircraft commodity group. Implementation of uniform capacity measurement for the other non-aircraft commodity groups will be contingent upon inclusion of paragraphs 2-4 through 2-12.

1-2 Terms Explained

a. Physical Capacity. The amount of workload, expressed in actual direct labor hours, that a facility can accommodate with all work positions manned on a single-shift, 5-day, 40-hour week basis while producing the product mix that the facility is designed to accommodate.

b. Peacetime Workloading Capacity. The amount of workload, expressed in actual direct labor hours, that a facility can effectively produce considering the management limitations upon applying sufficient workers to continuously fill every work position on a single-shift, 5-day, 40-hour week basis while producing the product mix that the facility is designed to accommodate.

c. <u>Work Position</u>. The designated space of equipment/process usage that can be occupied consistently by one direct production worker to accomplish the assigned task on a full-time basis. A work position may include more than one location if the worker moves to other locations to perform the assigned task.

d. <u>Work Station</u>. The lowest order of equipment/process location which requires separate analysis of work flow and function during the capacity calculation. It will consist of one or more work positions as determined by the criteria in paragraph 3-2b4.

e. <u>Shop</u>. This term refers to a work center, functional work group or resource group, etc. A shop generally represents the smallest organizational unit to which direct workers are assigned.

f. <u>Availability Factor</u>. The availability factor is the percentage of an 8-hour shift that a work station can be utilized to accomplish direct productive work. In cases where a facility is shared between depot maintenance and other activities/tenants, the availability factor may represent the percentage of an 8-hour shift the facility is available for the depot maintenance function.

g. <u>Depot Maintenance</u>. That maintenance which is the responsibility of and performed by designated maintenance activities, to augment stocks of serviceable materiel, and to support Organizational Maintenance and Intermediate Maintenance activities by the use of more extensive shop facilities, equipment, and personnel of higher technical skill than are available at the lower levels of maintenance. The phases normally consist of inspection, test, repair, modification, alteration, modernization, conversion, overhaul, reclamation or rebuild of parts, assemblies, subassemblies, components, equipment end items, and weapon systems; the manufacture of critical non-available parts; and providing technical assistance to using activities to using activities and intermediate maintenance organizations. Depot maintenance is normally accomplished in fixed shops, shipyards and other shore-based facilities, or by depot field teams.

h. <u>Direct Labor Factor</u>. That percentage of the 2000 hours of annual duty time per production employee which remains for direct application to the job after subtraction of leave, training and other recognized indirect hours.

i. <u>Production Shop Category (PSC)</u>. The segregation of, or identification of, maintenance shops consistent with the grouping(s) of materiel the shop is established and designed to process or produce. Ten PSC's specifically apply to aircraft. These are identified and fully explained in Chapter 2.

2

The PSC's for non-aircraft commodity groups are identified in DODI 4151.15.

    j. <u>Unutilized Space</u>. Unutilized space is that part of a plant capacity held in stand-by, idle or lay-away status.

    k. <u>Bottleneck</u>. A bottleneck is a process in the production flow within which capacity to do work is limited to the degree it restricts the ability to achieve full single, shift utilization of the other processes either preceding or following the bottleneck.

    l. <u>Product Mix</u>. A combination of heterogeneous workloads identified to major systems, subsystem components, stock classes, or items.

    m. <u>Commodity Group</u>. A grouping or range of items which possess similar characteristics, have similar applications, or are susceptible to similar logistics management methods.

1-3 <u>Objectives</u>

    a. To obtain a uniform measure of production capacity among the Services.

    b. To standardize capacity reporting methods among the Services, using applicable existing systems and procedures to the maximum extent possible.

    c. To collect credible and supportable capacity data.

    d. To maintain a capacity data base for planning applications by the Services and JADMAG.

    e. To provide validated capacity data inputs to the JADMAG Master Plan for analysis of plant utilization levels for mobilization and peacetime capabilities and to assess workload realignment recommendations.

    f. To provide validated capacity data to the Maintenance Interservice Support Management Offices (MISMOs) for their analysis and placement of workloads in consonance with the JADMAG Master Plan.

1-4 <u>Scope</u>

This publication provides the necessary guidance to implement a program whereby each military service will measure and report all depot maintenance capacity in a uniform manner. Reporting will be to JADMAG through respective command headquarters.

1-5 Responsibilities

    a. Each military service will:

        (1) Implement these procedures for production plant
capacity measurement and reporting.

        (2) Provide a focal point at each depot to ensure
proper measurement and reporting of production plant
capacity.

        (3) Provide a service focal point at each headquarters
to implement these procedures and to ensure accomplishment of
the objectives.

        (4) Revise its internal procedures as applicable to
accommodate these procedures and accomplishment of the
objectives.

        (5) Use the capacity data in the JADMAG Master Plan
for peacetime and mobilization capability planning.

    b. JADMAG will:

        (1) Collect capacity data in accordance with the JADMAG
Master Plan schedule and ensure application of the data in an
objective and uniform manner.

        (2) Maintain a central file of production plant
capacity.

        (3) Coordinate and monitor efforts of each service in
their measurement and reporting of capacity. Provide guidance
as required.

        (4) Establish and conduct on-site validation to ensure
uniformity, accuracy and credibility of the capacity data.

        (5) Report progress to the Joint Policy Coordinating
Group for Depot Maintenance Interservicing (JPCG-DMI) and the
JLC.

4

Chapter 2

Commodity Group Production Shop Categories

2-1 General

DODI 4151.15 identifies ten commodity groups. These commodity groups are segregated into Production Shop Categories consistent with the material the shops are established and designed to process or produce. For uniformity in reporting capacity, the definition of these categories has been expanded to include the identification of shops or work functions that are commonly assigned to each category. A ten digit code has been assigned to each shop or work function for reporting clarity.

2-2 Code Structure

The ten digit code used herein has been developed from existing service systems. The first digit is the commodity grouping as identified in DODI 4151.15. The second and third digits are the Production Shop Categories within the commodity group. The fourth, fifth, and sixth digits are from DODI 4165.3 and identify the facility class, category group, and basic category respectively. The seventh and eighth digits identify specific Navy facilities within the DOD basic categories as determined by NAVFAC P-72. Digits nine and ten identify specific Air Force facilities within the DOD basic categories using AFLCR 66-4, Chapter 5 as a basis.

2-3 Aircraft Production Shop Categories

101 Airframe. covered areas associated with processing the airframe under those programs commonly identified as Standard Depot Level Maintenance (SDLM), Programmed Depot Maintenance (PDM), On-Condition Maintenance (OCM), crash damage repair and/or overhaul, modernization, modification, etc. The work functions include cleaning, stripping, disassembly, airframe repair, reassembly, systems check, refinishing, painting, and fueling/defueling using covered facilities.

101-211-1190   o   Shop, Corrosion Control. (This category includes aircraft corrosion control and decontamination facilities designed for cleaning, paint stripping, etc., of the complete aircraft.)

101-211-126F   o   Paint and Finishing Hangar.

101-211-133B   o   Shop, Nondestructive Inspection. (This category applies to shop space used for nondestructive inspection of Airframes.)

101-211-141A   o   Shop, Machine (Airframe Dedicated). (Facility dedicated to support airframe requirements only.)

101-211-141B   o   Shop, Welding (Airframe Dedicated). (Facility dedicated to support airframe requirements only.)

101-211-141C   o   Shop, Plating (Airframe Dedicated). (Facility dedicated to support airframe requirements only.)

101-211-141I   o   Shop, Airframe Examination and Evaluation, Pre-Shop Analysis and Examination and Inspection.

101-211-1430   o   Dock, Maintenance. (Applicable to structures which normally cover only a portion of the aircraft.)

101-211-144S   o   Shop, Quick Engine Change. (A facility used for quick engine change and engine build-up including deseal and reseal operations.)

101-211-146B   o   Shop, Aircraft Overhaul and Repair. (Trainers, Attack Fighters and Helicopters.)

101-211-146E   o   Shop, Aircraft Overhaul and Repair. (Bombers, Cargo and Patrol.)

101-211-1490   o   Dock, Maintenance. (Fuel System Facility).

102. _Engine_. covered areas associated with processing jet, turbojet, and reciprocating type aviation engines in terms of overhaul, low time repair, complete repair, and major inspection. The work functions include uncanning, disassembly, cleaning, material examination, parts reconditioning, subassembly, final assembly and preservation.

102-211-2260   o   Shop, Engine Preparation and Storage. (Areas used in preparing the engines for test, storage or shipment.)

102-211-233B   o   Shop, Nondestructive Testing (Engines).

102-211-237I   o   Shop, Engine Examination and Evaluation, Pre-Shop Analysis, Examination and Inspection.

102-211-241A   o   Shop, Cleaning (Engine Dedicated).

6

102-211-241B   o Shop, Paint (Engine Dedicated).

102-211-241C   o Shop, Machine (Engine Dedicated).

102-211-241D   o Shop, Plating (Engine Dedicated).

102-211-241E   o Shop, Welding (Engine Dedicated).

102-211-247D   o Shop, Engine Modification and Repair. (All
                   type Engines).

102-211-257A   o Shop, Jet Engine Overhaul.

102-211-267B   o Shop, Reciprocating Engine Overhaul.

102-211-277C   o Shop, Turbine Engine Overhaul.

103. Accessories and Components. Covered areas associated with
processing airframe and engine accessories.

103-211-311A   o Shop, Cleaning (Dedicated).

103-211-311B   o Shop, Paint (Dedicated).

103-211-311C   o Shop, Machine (Dedicated).

103-211-311D   o Shop, Plating (Dedicated).

103-211-311E   o Shop, Welding (Dedicated).

103-211-313E   o Shop, Examination and Evaluation, Pre-shop
                   Analysis, Examination and Inspection.

103-211-314A   o Shop, Hazardous Test. (Facility used to test
                   a portion of the accessories items overhauled
                   above. Because of the volatile fluid with which
                   they are tested or the hazardous conditions of
                   testing, the test area must be rigidly
                   controlled. Items such as fuel pumps, fuel
                   controls, etc. are worked in this area.)

103-211-314B   o Shop, Reclamation (Facility for removal of
                   useable parts from defective end item
                   components).

103-211-3140   o Shop, Aircraft and Engine Accessories
                   Overhaul. (Facility used for the overhaul and
                   testing of miscellaneous accessories such as
                   control assemblies, engine fuel system
                   components, accessories gear drives.)

103-211-324D   o   Shop, Tank and Radiator Repair. (Facility to repair all types of radiators, inter-coolers and metal tanks.)

103-211-327A   o   Shop, Sheet Metal. (Facility for repair of surface sheet metal parts.)

103-211-327S   o   Shop, Metal Surface. (Facility for repair of wings, doors, stabilizers, tailbooms, control surfaces, etc.).

103-211-328S   o   Shop, Seat Repair.

103-211-328M   o   Shop, Metal Bonding.

103-211-328N   o   Shop, Container Reclamation. (Facility for repair of engine, transmission, rotor blade and other type metal containers.)

103-211-332L   o   Shop, Life Raft Repair. (Includes inflatable life vests, dinghies, etc.)

103-211-332N   o   Shop, Rubber Repair. (Facility for the repair of rubber equipment such as aircraft fuel cells and molded rubber products.)

103-211-334B   o   Shop, Parachute Repair. (Facility for repair of parachutes, aerial pickup gear, etc.).

103-211-334G   o   Shop, Fabric and Upholstery.

103-211-334L   o   Shop, Tire Repair.

103-211-335A   o   Shop, Plastic and Fiberglass. (Facility for the repair of fiberglass and reinforced plastic items such as radomes, wingtips, ducts, covers, canopies, hatches and windows).

103-211-338N   o   Shop, Composite rework.

103-211-344F   o   Shop, Propeller and Propeller Control Overhaul.

103-211-347B   o   Shop, Rotor Head Overhaul.

103-211-347C   o   Shop, Rotor Blade Overhaul.

103-211-348A   o   Shop, Transmission/Gearbox Overhaul.

103-211-348B   o   Shop, Dynamic Drive System Overhaul. (Facility used for the repair of drive shafts, pitch links, swash plates, etc.)

103-211-354C   o   Shop, Hydraulic Components Overhaul. (Facility used to overhaul hydraulic components.)

103-211-3540   o   Shop, Bearings. (This category designates a specialized shop in which bearings are cleaned, disassembled, inspected, reassembled and tested.)

103-211-354U   o   Shop, Aircraft Landing Gear. (Facility used for the repair and overhaul of aircraft landing gear components such as wheels, brakes and struts.)

103-211-363A   o   Shop, Alternator Drive Overhaul. (Facilities for the repair of alternator drive components.)

103-211-364E   o   Shop, Electrical Accessories Overhaul and Test. (Facility used in the overhaul and test of electrical components including electrical systems, starters, control equipment and converters, etc.)

103-211-364Q   o   Shop, Battery. (A facility for the repair and test of aircraft batteries.)

103-211-364S   o   Shop, Constant Speed Drive.

103-211-365E   o   Shop, Electro-Mechanical Components. (Facility used to repair Electro-Mechanical actuators, cargo and rescue hoists, etc.)

103-211-371A   o   Shop, Turbine Accessories Overhaul. (The primary workload in this category is air compressor type equipment, such as air turbine starters, air conditioning packs, and air driven motors.)

103-211-371B   o   Shop, Turbine Accessories Test.

103-211-371E   o   Shop, General Purpose Units. (This includes the overhaul and repair of gas/air turbine engines and auxiliary power units, installed on the aircraft other than its' primary propulsion unit.)

103-211-371F   o   Shop, General Purpose Units Tests.

103-211-372A   o   Shop, Ram/Air Turbine Accessories Overhaul. (Air driven accessories such as ram air turbines, scoops).

103-211-372B   o   Shop, Ram/Air Turbine Accessories Test.

103-211-385C   o   Shop, Pneumatic Components Overhaul. (Facility used to overhaul pneumatic components.)

103-211-389A   o   Shop, Cryogenics.

103-211-384M   o   Shop, Oxygen Equipment. (Facility used for repair of oxygen regulators, converters, etc.)

103-211-394N   o   Shop, Photographic Equipment Repair. (Facility for repair of aircraft cameras and other photographic items).

103-211-394P   o   Shop, Optical Component Repair.

104.   <u>Electronic, Communication and Armament Systems</u>. Covered areas associated with processing airborne communication and navigation equipment, instruments, airborne data computers, fire control and bombing system equipment, gyroscopes, inertial guidance systems, and other avionics equipment.

104-211-411A   o   Shop, Cleaning (Dedicated).

104-211-411B   o   Shop, Paint (Dedicated).

104-211-411C   o   Shop, Machine (Dedicated).

104-211-411D   o   Shop, Welding (Dedicated).

104-211-411E   o   Shop, Plating (Dedicated).

104-211-411F   o   Shop, Bearings (Dedicated).

104-211-4110   o   Shop, Instrument Overhaul.

104-211-4220   o   Shop, Armament and Avionics. (Facility for repair of navigational missile and bombing radar; electronic countermeasure equipment; flight facilities and communication equipment; electronic instruments, and fire control systems.)

104-211-4230   o   Shop, Airborne Systems Software. (Facility for preparation, repair or modification of software packages for aircraft automated systems).

104-211-4260   o   Shop, Navigational Aids Repair. (Facility for repair of airborne navigational instruments such as celestial tracking system, sextants, driftmeters, etc.)

104-211-4270   o   Shop, Avionics Testing.

104-211-431E   o   Shop, Inertial Quality Gyroscope Overhaul.
               (Environmentally controlled space for the overhaul
               of inertial quality gyroscopes. Inertial quality
               gyroscopes are those having a radome drift rate of
               0.25 degrees per hour or less. All other
               gyroscopes are considered non-inertial quality for
               facility categorization purposes.)

104-211-431G   o   Shop, Inertial Guidance System Overhaul and
               Calibration.

104-211-441B   o   Shop, Electronic Instrument Overhaul.
               (Facility used to support
               communications electronic instruments such as
               systems and display panels, oscilloscopes, etc..)

104-211-441C   o   Shop, Mechanical Instrument Overhaul.
               (Facility for overhaul of items such as bank
               indicators and air speed indicators.)

104-211-441D   o   Shop, Non-inertial Gyroscope Overhaul.
               (Facility used to overhaul non-inertial gyroscope
               devices such as N-1 compass gyroscopes, bomb
               navigational system gyroscopes, etc.)

104-211-441H   o   Shop, Magnetic Instrument Overhaul and Test.

105. Armament. Covered areas associated with processing
weapons including guns, missiles, bomb racks, weapon pylons,
etc., used by the aircraft in carrying out its assigned
mission.

105-211-511A   o   Shop, Cleaning (Dedicated).

105-211-511B   o   Shop, Paint (Dedicated).

105-211-511C   o   Shop, Machine (Dedicated).

105-211-511D   o   Shop, Welding (Dedicated).

105-211-511E   o   Shop, Plating (Dedicated).

105-211-5230   o   Shop, Aircraft Weapon Overhaul and Test.

105-211-5240   o   Shop, Ordnance Equipment.

105-211-5250   o   Shop, Weapon Accessories Repair. (Facility
               for repair of bomb racks, weapon pylons,
               etc.)

105-211-5320   o   Shop, Missile. (Facility for repair of air launched missiles.)

106.   Support Equipment. Covered areas associated with processing aviation general and special support equipment and aerospace ground support equipment.

106-211-611A   o   Shop, Cleaning (Dedicated).

106-211-611B   o   Shop, Paint (Dedicated).

106-211-611C   o   Shop, Machine (Dedicated).

106-211-611D   o   Shop, Plating (Dedicated).

106-211-611E   o   Shop, Welding (Dedicated).

106-211-6210   o   Shop, Aeronautical Electronic Support Equipment. (Includes mobile maintenance facility construction, outfitting and repair.)

106-211-621V   o   Shop, Electronic Test Systems Repair. (Facility for repair of VAST, ATE, etc.)

106-211-6280   o   Shop, Precision Measurement Equipment. (Facility used to repair, calibrate and certify precision measurement and test equipment. Type III).

106-211-6320   o   Shop, GSE Maintenance. (Facility for servicing and maintaining ground support equipment such as, workstands, fire fighting equipment, portable air conditioners, air compressors, generators, etc.)

106-211-632M   o   Shop, Training Devices. (Facility used to repair, and modify training aids such as, mock ups, cut away models, etc.)

106-211-634R   o   Shop, Hydrostatics. (Facility used to periodically inspect and overhaul of hydrostatic equipment.)

106-211-641H   o   Shop, Ground Support Equipment Holding Shed.

107.   Manufacture and Repair. Covered areas which are not an integral part of other categories previously described and which contribute to aircraft repair operations by such work functions as parts cleaning and painting, plating and metal processing shop.

12

107-211-712G   o Shop, Welding.

107-211-712H   o Shop, Foundry.

107-211-712X   o Shop, Peening and Blasting.

107-211-713B   o Shop, Nondestructive Inspection. (Magnetic
                  particle, Dye Pentrant, etc.)

107-211-716A   o Shop, Parts Cleaning.

107-211-716B   o Shop, Parts Painting.

107-211-722D   o Shop, Machine.

107-211-722S   o Shop, Grinding. (Facility used primarily for
                  close tolerance grinding of metal parts that have
                  been built up by metalizing or electroplating
                  processes.)

107-211-722U   o Shop, NC Machine. (Facility primarily using
                  numerically controlled machines; separate from
                  common machine shop.)

107-211-722Y   o Shop, Metal Parts Fabrication.

107-211-732C   o Shop, Metal Processing. (Facility for metal
                  treating processes such as nickel braze, ceramic
                  coating, plasma, etc.)

107-211-732E   o Shop, Plating.

107-211-732F   o Shop, Heat Treating. (Facility for heat
                  treating metals such as, tempering, annealing,
                  quenching, stress relieving, etc.)

107-211-742J   o Shop, Plastic Fabrication. (Facility for the
                  manufacture of plastic items such as, tubing,
                  caps, covers, panels, foam container liners,
                  templates, fixtures and tooling.)

107-211-742L   o Shop, Pattern.

107-211-742M   o Shop, Decal (Graphic Arts)

107-211-742P   o Shop, Woodworking.

107-211-744A   o Shop, Rubber Fabrication. (Facility for
                  fabrication of rubber equipment, such as
                  aircraft fuel cells and molded rubber
                  products.)

107-211-765B o Shop, Tubing.

107-211-765C o Shop, Cable.

107-211-765D o Shop, Cordage (Flight Controls).

107-211-765E o Shop, Electrical Cable/Harness

108. _Test and Calibration_. Covered areas which are dedicated to test, trim, or calibrate engines, electronics, communications or armament systems.

108-211-833B o Jet Engine Test Cell. (10,000-16,000 lbs. maximum thrust.)

108-211-833C o Jet Engine Test Cell. (Over -16,000 lbs. maximum thrust.)

108-211-833D o Jet Engine Test Stand. (Facility for testing jet aircraft engines, which has no accoustical noise abatement and is not part of an enclosed facility.)

108-211-833E o Turbo Prop Test Cell.

108-211-833F o Reciprocating Engine Test Cell. (3,000 HP or less.)

108-211-833G o Reciprocating Engine Test Cell. (Over 3,000 HP.)

108-211-833H o Reciprocating Engine Test Stand. (Facility for testing reciprocating aircraft engines, which has no accoustical noise abatement and is not part of an enclosed facility.)

108-211-833I o Turbo Shaft Test Cell.

108-211-833J o Turbo Fan Test Cell.

108-211-833K o Pneumatic Gas/Air Turbine Test Cell.

108-211-8440 o Helicopter Blade Test Facility.

108-211-8560 o Radome Test Facility.

108-211-8660 o Radar/Antenna Test Facility.

108-211-8700 o Aircraft Bore Sight Range.

14

109. <u>Other</u>. Those areas used to perform productive work that are not included in categories 1 through 8 above. This includes ramp, apron, and aircraft storage sites.

109-211-9110   o   Apron, Aircraft Rework (Uncovered areas specifically assigned for depot maintenance.)

109-211-911A   o   Apron, Reclamation (Uncovered areas assigned to depot maintenance used for performing aircraft reclamation work.)

109-211-911B   o   Pad, Armament and Disarmament.

109-211-911C   o   Apron, Predock/Postdock.

109-211-9120   o   Aircraft Corrosion Control Facility (Uncovered).

109-211-913A   o   Ground Check/Flight Test Support (Uncovered).

109-211-921A   o   Ground Check/Flight Test Support (Covered).

109-211-934A   o   Material Handlers/Parts Expediters.

109-211-935A   o   Material Control Laboratory.

109-211-935B   o   Standards Laboratory.

109-211-936A   o   Programmer's (Automatic Test Equipment and Numerical Controlled Machine.)

109-211-9440   o   Power Check Pad (No Suppressor)

109-211-9450   o   Power Check Pad with Suppressor.

109-211-9460   o   Propeller Aircraft Power Check Pad.

109-211-9470   o   Helicopter Aircraft Power Check Pad.

109-211-9480   o   VSTOL Aircraft Power Check

109-211-9510   o   Packaging and Preservation

109-211-980G   o   Aircraft Power Check Facility (Covered facility which encloses the entire aircraft and contains sound suppression equipment.)

110. <u>General Shop Support</u>. Those covered spaces which are used in providing general support to all aircraft production operations. General support includes functions such as management, supervision, engineering, clerical functions, plant maintenance, central or general storage, quality assurance, and

materials testing. This category includes offices, cafeterias, supervisors' work space, shop parts storage areas, multipurpose/main aisles, wash and dressing areas, dispatching facilities, inspection facilities, stairwells, auxillary equipment rooms, walls, etc.

> NOTE: Codes for subdivisions of this category are defined in the instructions for completing JLC Form 26 "Reporting of General Shop Support."

*2-4   <u>Missile Production Shop Categories</u>

*2-5   <u>Ships Production Shop Categories</u>

*2-6   <u>Combat Vehicles Production Shop Categories</u>

*2-7   <u>Automotive Equipment Production Shop Categories</u>

*2-8   <u>Construction Equipment Production Shop Categories</u>

*2-9   <u>Electronic and Communications Systems Production Shop Categories</u>

*2-10 <u>Ordnance, Weapons and Munitions Production Shop Categories</u>

*2-11 <u>Generator Set Production Shop Categories</u>

*2-12 <u>General Purpose Equipment Production Shop Categories</u>

*Use codes identified in DODI 4151.15 until detailed breakout is added.

16

Chapter 3

CAPACITY MEASUREMENT

3-1 General

    a. Although the techniques in this publication are oriented toward capacity measurement of covered shop space, they can be applied to uncovered areas used in depot operations. For example, the techniques are appropriate for measurement of the capacity of uncovered test and calibration areas. Unless otherwise directed, uncovered work areas and those areas included in the Production Shop Categories titled "other" and "general shop support" are not to be included in the capacity measurement calculations.

    b. Two factors govern the capacity to accomplish depot maintenance of material. The facility, its included shop equipment, and product mix establish the physical capacity. The ability to place the necessary work force skills on the job when needed establishes the peacetime workloading capacity. Both need to be determined before programming workloads or calculating facility utilization. This guidance specifies techniques for determining both.

3-2 Physical Capacity

    a. Physical Capacity may be limited by the shop availability factor and/or the bottlenecks. Calculation of the availability factor is addressed in Chapter 4. Treatment for bottlenecks is addressed in paragraph 3-2b5.

    b. The following steps provide the procedure for calculating physical capacity. It is necessary to follow these procedures for each shop as a separate reporting entity.

        1. Determine the product mix the shop is required to accommodate.

        2. Prepare a detailed shop layout which identifies the shop function, boundaries, area, work stations, work positions, and specific equipment/work bench locations.

        3. The number of work positions identified on the layout should reflect the maximum number that can be effectively and efficiently utilized to accomplish the assigned product mix. In determining the maximum number, the following rationale applies:

            (a) Equipment identified on the layout must be in place and operational at the time the shop capacity is measured to be included in the work position count.

(b) Work benches must be in place or readily available to set in place and made operational within one (1) day where power, air and utilities, if required, are already available to be included in the work position count. Typically this demonstrates a situation where the equipment has been disconnected and set aside for the convenience of the shop or because existing workload does not require its use.

(c) Mobile type work stands and equipment must be on hand, available for immediate relocation to the position identified on the layout, and functionally operational to be included in the work position count.

(d) The shop layout prepared for purposes of capacity determination should reflect a realistic configuration of the shop. The layout should not portray conditions which include equipment, work benches, and mobile stands that are not available and/or cannot readily be made operational or require a major shop rearrangement to conform with the layout.

(e) The removal, installation, or relocation of equipment/work benches, etc., constitutes a reconfiguration which may affect the shop capacity. A shop layout prepared for the "new" configuration should not be used for capacity measurement unless action to reconfigure is physically in progress at the time the capacity determination is made.

4. Work station capacity is governed by the following rationale:

(a) If the equipment/process in the work station is designed to be operated by one person, the capacity shall be recorded as one work position.

(b) If the equipment/process in the work station is designed to be operated by more than one person, the capacity is the number of work positions that these personnel represent.

(c) If the equipment/process is infrequently used by a person(s) from one or more work stations, it will be designated as support equipment and not included as a capacity work position, e.g., a drill press used occasionally by several workers.

(d) If an equipment/process is frequently but not continuously utilized, it should be included as part of another related position and not counted as a separate work position for capacity, e.g., a cleaning device used frequently by one mechanic principally working at an equipment/bench site.

18

(e) If a work position is designed to be manned continuously but is currently vacant because of reduced workload quantity, it shall be counted as capacity.

(f) Some examples of work stations are:

(1) Stall/Work Bay/Aircraft Dock. For the stall/work bay/aircraft dock (or assembly line spot) situation, the number of persons who can effectively work during each phase of the process cycle will be determined. Chapter 4 addresses a method for performing this calculation. In general, the weighted average over the cycle is used as the work position quantity of the work station. An analysis of a product mix and process variations may be necessary to determine this value. The cycle or "flow time" in the stall/work bay/aircraft dock/assembly line spot should be the cycle which would exist under optimum conditions for the designated product mix. Inordinately long cycle times due to current non-availability of material, manpower, etc. - should be shortened to suit the intent of the definition of physical capacity, i.e., capacity unconstrained by a current lack of material or manpower.

(2) Major Special Facilities (Engine Test Cell, Radar Range, Helicopter Rotor Test Aircraft, Power Check Facility, etc.). These special facilities should be assigned work positions reflecting designed utilization of the facility, i.e., handled similar to work positions referred to in paragraph 3-2b4(f)(1) (above).

(3) Bulk Processing Area (Plating, Chemical Cleaning, Heat Treating, etc.). Bulk processing work stations, where design is largely determined by required product mix, can be regarded as one work station with capacity determined by the number of persons necessary to effectively man the entire work station.

(4) Bench (hydraulics, Electronics, etc.). A work station in a bench type operation may consist of one or more work benches and support equipment items. A work bench designated for continuous productive activity will be counted as a work position.

(5) Equipment (Machine Tools, Component Test Stands, etc.). Equipment work stations may include one or more items of equipment and be assigned one or more work positions depending on the designed utilization of each item of equipment within the station.

5. Analysis for bottlenecks which limit work flow between work stations should be conducted when the detailed shop layout is prepared. The bottleneck should be eliminated through appropriate

techniques to achieve a balanced work level among all work stations as required to accommodate the workload. If the bottleneck cannot be eliminated, the Industrial Engineer or Technician must consider that particular operation/process as the pacing factor. The work station and work position designations must be limited to only that number required to accommodate maximum utilization of the bottleneck operation/process. Only these positions are to be indicated on the layout. In practice every flow process has a pacing operation/process which the engineer or technician routinely considers in preparing shop layouts. In other words, proper preparation of the shop layout will suffice for the treatment of bottlenecks and a special method over and above standard engineering practices is not required.

6. Multiply the number of work positions in each work station by 2000 to obtain the gross capacity expressed in manhours.

7. Multiply the gross capacity obtained in step 6 above by the availability factor. (Use .95 unless some other specific availability factor can be justified using JLC Form 23 in Chapter 4. When completing the form, provide sufficient detail so that the computations are clear and easily followed.)

8. Add the capacities of the work stations to arrive at a physical capacity for each shop and identify the shop to a PSC (ten digit code). (Do not split shops into two or more Production Shop Categories.) However, if a shop performs work in two or more sub-category codes (ten digit code level) within a PSC, that portion of the capacity associated within that specific shop. Next, summarize shop capacities to derive the depot capacity for each Production Shop Category. The resulting totals comprise the depots' current single-shift physical capacity unadjusted for manpower availability.

3-3 Peacetime Workloading Capacity

a. Full single-shift utilization of each work position requires the proper skill to be working the position for 2,000 hours of direct labor per year. Leave, training, and miscellaneous indirect factors as described in DOD 7220.29H preclude obtaining 2,000 hours of direct labor from an individual worker.

b. The alternatives for utilization are: (1) to have one worker per work position and expect to have positions unmanned when workers are absent, or (2) to obtain more workers than there are work positions and fill all vacant positions from a pool of extra workers. Peacetime needs for the most cost effective operation favor the first alternative. Surge or wartime situations, where the volume of production could be more important than the cost considerations, tend to favor the second alternative to the extent that trained workers can be generated.

c. When warranted by the required volume of production, work stations and shops may be operated under the second alternative during peacetime. For example, workers can be dispatched as needed from a skill pool to an aircraft dock or similar function. Sufficient skilled workers are kept on the payroll to ensure that workers are available to man all work positions each day. This practice is common when the flow time on the equipment being repaired must be kept within the shortest possible time.

d. This section provides guidance for calculating peacetime workloading capacity under both alternatives. The steps are repeated in a flow chart on page 22.

1. Obtain the physical capacity in accordance with paragraph 3-2.

2. Determine whether sufficient workers are hired to regularly man the available work positions.

(a) If the answer is yes, the second alternative situation exists and the physical capacity is also the peacetime workloading capacity.

(b) If the answer is no, proceed to step 3.

(c) If the answer is between yes and no, a judgment must be made to determine what percentage of the capacity should be treated in accordance with step 2a and what percentage should be treated in accordance with step 2b.

3. From data gathered in accordance with the provisions of DOD 7220.29H determine the direct labor hours that have been received from the workers assigned to the function under review.

4. Divide the direct labor hours by 2,000 hours per year to obtain the direct labor factor.

5. Multiply the direct labor factor by the physical capacity to determine the peacetime workloading capacity.

3-4 Direct and Indirect Functions

a. Typically, only those shop functions assigned as direct are included in the capacity determination. The assignment of direct functions varies among the services and in some cases

22

between depots within a service. For purposes of capacity measurement, in accordance with this publication to accommodate these variances, the following specific direct/indirect functional assignments are to be used for the aircraft commodity group.

    b. Direct Functions

        1. Quality inspection stations within a shop.

        2. Examination and Evaluation (E&E), Examination and Inspection (E&I), and Pre-shop Analysis (PSA) within a production shop.

        3. Snappers/team leaders within a shop.

        4. Nondestructive testing performed within a production shop.

    c. Indirect Functions (These functions may be reported in PSC 109 or PSC 110).

        1. Material/Chemical/Metallurgy/Metrology laboratory personnel.

        2. Crane operators that service two (2) or more shops.

        3. Material handlers/parts expediters who assemble, deliver, and preposition repair parts and supplies for subsequent use.

        4. First-line supervisor.

        5. Automatic test equipment and numerically controlled machine programmers (if not an integral part of a production shop).

        6. Packaging and preservation.

        7. Test Pilots.

    NOTE: Direct and indirect functional assignments for other commodity groups will be included at a later date.

3-5. _Unutilized Space_

    a. Unutilized space in the custody of the reporting depot maintenance activity can represent potential production capacity. If placement of the proper equipment in such space is feasible within the ensuing year and would enable the space to be made productive then it should be counted as potential capacity. This capacity will be reported separately as specified in Chapter 4.

b.   The capacity of the unutilized space may be estimated as follows: (1) Determine the process or product the facility is most suited to accommodate and select the applicable commodity group and Production Shop Category, and (2) divide the area of the unutilized space by the average square feet required per work position in the Production Shop Category selected. The result is the estimated capacity.

c.   It must be emphasized that unutilized space is only that space within the depot maintenance activity held in standby, idle or lay-away status. Unmanned positions or idle space within an active shop represents underutilized capacity rather than unutilized capacity. Underutilized capacity should reported integral with the cognizant shop.

3-6   Non-Aeronautical Commodity Groups

Those areas where non-aeronautical maintenance functions are predominant in a shop and performed within an aeronautical depot will have capacity measured and reported within the commodity group assignment in accordance with DODI 4151.15. The Production Shop Category codes shown in paragraph 2-3 are for the aircraft commodity group only.

24

Chapter 4

Capacity Reporting

4-1 <u>General</u>

a. The physical and peacetime capacity of each aeronautical maintenance depot will be reported to JADMAG annually. The specific reporting dates for any given year will be established by JADMAG and a tasking directive issued as required to obtain the data. Capacity data for other than aircraft commodity groups will be reported as directed by individual service headquarters.

b. This chapter outlines the reporting procedures for capacity. JLC Form 21 is used to summarize capacity data by depot. JLC Form 22 will be prepared for each shop performing direct functions that require capacity measurement. JLC Forms 23 and 24 will be prepared when applicable. JLC Form 25 will be used for reporting unutilized space. JLC Form 26 will be prepared for each area where indirect functions are performed.

c. A copy of all prepared forms will be submitted to JADMAG. Copies of each form and additional supporting/back-up data such as shop layouts, labor standards, etc., will be maintained on file at the depot. These will be made available to JADMAG personnel or representatives thereof at such time as an on-site validation is conducted.

d. The following Report Control Symbols have been assigned to the reporting requirements listed:

    (1) NAVMAT 4790-7 Depot Maintenance Capacity Data Summary (JLC Form 21)

    (2) NAVMAT 4790-8 Depot Maintenance Shop Capacity Calculation (JLC Form 22)

    (3) NAVMAT 4790-9 Depot Maintenance Shop Availability Factor Calculation (JLC Form 23)

    (4) NAVMAT 4790-10 Depot Maintenance Stall/Work Bay/ Dock/Assembly Line Capacity Calculation (JLC Form 24)

    (5) NAVMAT 4790-11 Unutilized Shop Support (JLC Form 25)

    (6) NAVMAT 4790-13 General Shop Support (JLC Form 26)

INSTRUCTION FOR PREPARATION
OF "DEPOT MAINTENANCE CAPACITY DATA SUMMARY"
JLC FORM 21

1. General

    JLC Form 21 expresses the depots' capacity by Production
    Shop Category as summed from the aggregate of shops in each
    category.

2. Elements 1 through 6   Complete these as indicated - self
                                  explanatory

3. Columns A and B   Enter the physical capacity and
                                  peacetime capacity summed from
                                  Blocks L and N respectively of JLC
                                  Form 22

    Note: This form is applicable only to the aircraft
           commodity group.

26

JLC FORM 21 OCT 81

DEPOT MAINTENANCE
CAPACITY DATA SUMMARY

1 - DEPOT NAME	2 - DEPOT CODE	3 - PREPARED BY	4 - ORGANIZATION	5 - PHONE	6 - DATE

CODE	PRODUCTION SHOP CATEGORY	UTILIZED SPACE		
		PHYSICAL CAPACITY A	PEACETIME CAPACITY B	
101	AIR FRAMES	MH	MH	
102	ENGINES	MH	MH	
103	AIRCRAFT AND ENGINES ACCESSORIES AND COMPONENTS	MH	MH	
104	ELECTRONIC & COMMUNICATION EQUIPMENT	MH	MH	
105	ARMAMENT	MH	MH	
106	SUPPORT EQUIPMENT	MH	MH	
107	MANUFACTURE AND REPAIR	MH	MH	
108	TEST & CALIBRATION	MH	MH	
	TOTAL	MH	MH	
109	OTHER	MH	MH	
110	GENERAL SHOP SUPPORT	SF	SF	
	NON - AERONAUTICAL	MH	MH	

SAMPLE

INSTRUCTIONS FOR PREPARATION
OF "DEPOT MAINTENANCE SHOP CAPACITY CALCULATION"
JLC FORM 22

1. General

    The shop capacity is the denominator of the formula used to
    compute utilization of DOD Facilities. Capacity data
    reported by the Services may be used in evaluating future
    workload distribution and for interservice decisions.
    Therefore, careful attention must be given the development
    of accurate and current data. JLC Form 22 provides a
    uniform approach to document and report capacity. The form
    is developed to fit the DOD 4151.15H criteria.

2. Elements 1 through 7   Complete these as indicated - self
                                  explanatory.

3. Block A   Enter the alpha or numeric code
                                  representing the identity of the
                                  depot entered in Element 1 (left
                                  justify the entry).

4. Block B   Enter the building number in which
                                  the shop identified in element 2
                                  is located. If a shop is located in
                                  more than one building, enter the
                                  building number representing the
                                  greatest portion of the floor
                                  spaces and place an "S" behind the
                                  building number to indicate the
                                  shop is split between buildings.
                                  Explain split shops in remarks
                                  block - i.e. 60% of shop X is in
                                  Building A and 40% in Building B.

                                  NOTE: A separate form for each
                                         building may be prepared and
                                         submitted if desired.
                                         (Right justify the entry).

5. Block C   Enter the shop alpha or numeric
                                  identifier (left justify the
                                  entry).

6. Block D   Enter the ten digit number
                                  representing the Production Shop
                                  Category and Facility Category
                                  Code applicable to the shop.
                                  Reference Chapter 2 for the
                                  facility codes.

7. Block E   Enter the shop name, i.e., Landing
                               Gear, Plating, Bearing, etc., (left
                               justify the entry).

8. Block F   Enter the drawing number of the
                               layout for the shop identified in
                               Block C (left justify the entry).

9. Block G   Enter the total gross square feet
                               of the shop identified in Block C.
                               This number must correspond to that
                               computed from the layout drawing
                               (right justify the entry).

10. Block H   Within the spaces allocated,
                               provide a brief listing of the items
                               worked in the shop and associated
                               weapon system i.e., - Landing
                               Gear F-14 (left justify the
                               entry).

11. Block I   Enter the total number of work
                               positions identified in the shop
                               when determining the physical
                               capacity of the shop (right
                               justify the entry).

12. Block J   Enter the gross capacity in
                               manhours using a 2000
                               manhour/year/position factor
                               (right justify the entry).

13. Block K   Enter the availability factor of
                               .95 or that computed from JLC
                               Form 23 (right justify the
                               entry). Attach JLC Form 23
                               as back up.

14. Block L   Compute and enter the physical
                               capacity (right justify the
                               entry).

15. Block M   Enter the direct labor factor
                               rounded off to the nearest 1,000th
                               (right justify the entry).

16. Block N   Enter the peacetime capacity - self
                               explanatory (multiply blocks L&M)
                               (right justify the entry).

17. All forms shall be signed and dated by the
supervisor of the organization identified in Element 4.

18. Insert remarks as necessary on the bottom section of the
form.

30

INSTRUCTION FOR PREPARATION
OF "SHOP AVAILABILITY FACTOR CALCULATION"
JLC FORM 23

1. General

    Use of this form is only necessary when the standard
    availability factor of .95 is not used. An availability
    factor must be determined for each shop and the shop
    identified to a predominant PSC.

2. Elements 1   Complete these as indicated on
    through 11   the form - self-explanatory.

3. Column A   Enter the numerical sequence
                                of work stations identified in the
                                shop. The work stations must also
                                be identified on a current shop
                                layout.

4. Columns B, C, D,   Enter the average annual downtime
    E and F   in hours for the equipment in the
                                work station for Preventive
                                Maintenance (PM), Calibration
                                (CAL), Unscheduled
                                Maintenance (UM) and Warm-Up
                                (W-UP).

5. Column G   Enter the total of Columns B
                                through F.

6. Column H   Enter the total number of work
                                positions in each work station as
                                identified when computing
                                physical capacity.

7. Column I, J, K,   Complete these as indicated on the
    and Blocks L, M,   form. The number computed and
    and N   entered in Block N represents the
                                availability factor for the shop
                                identified in Element 3.

8. Equipment identified as support to a work station will not
be included in the availability factor computation unless its
downtime controls the production of that or another work
station.

32

METHOD FOR DETERMINING
CAPACITY OF STALL/WORK BAY/DOCK/ASSEMBLY LINE SPOT
JLC FORM 24

1. General

   Airframe capacity measurement requires a detailed analysis
   of the tasks to be performed during each operation/phase of
   the maintenance cycle. From this analysis the flow/cycle
   time must be determined. The combination of manhours
   required, number of work positions and flow/cycle time
   determines the capacities for each operation. The sum of
   The sum of capacities for each operation
   multiplied by the number of airframe work stations available
   equals the total airframe capacity. JLC Form 24 provides a
   systematic method of recording the tasks, manhours, work
   positions and flow/cycle time for computing airframe capacity
   and serves as supporting documentation for review and
   verification. To expedite use of the form, and simplify
   reporting, it is acceptable to combine all tasks for a
   specific shop with corresponding total manhours and flowtime
   indicated and the work positions computed from Block G
   entered in Block I of JLC Form 22. Supporting documentation
   for the manhours and flowtime must be maintained in the depot
   files for review by JADMAG.

   In many cased, several shops may simultaneously perform
   work on an aircraft in a dock/stall. In this situation, it
   is necessary to prorate the total capacity of the dock/stall
   to each of the applicable shops and report a capacity for
   each shop.

   Use of this form is applicable to all commodity groups
   though the instructions are oriented to aircraft. Broadening
   of the instructions to more specifically address the other
   commodity groups is contingent upon incorporation of
   paragraphs 2-4 through 2-12.

2. Elements   Complete these as indicated - self
   1 through 11   explanatory.

3. Block A   Insert the applicable operation and
                               weapons system. Typical airframe
                               repair operations are: Disassembly,
                               Electrical Repairs/Checks,
                               Hydraulic and Pneumatic Repairs/
                               Checks, Structural Repairs, Sheet
                               Metal Repairs/Rework, and Assembly.
                               Other operations may also apply.

4. Block B   Identify all tasks required for each
                               operation in the sequence they
                               should be performed.

NOTE: All tasks may be
combined for a specific work
center/shop as explained in
center/shop as explained in
paragraph 1.

5. Block C   Enter the manhour standard or
estimated time required to
complete the corresponding task in
Block B.

6. Block D   Enter the total number of work
positions for each task in Block B
as determined when computing
physical capacity. NOTE: When
all tasks/manhours/and flowtimes
are combined, this block is
omitted.

7. Block E   The number of positions (Block
D) multiplied by eight (8) is the
total number of manhours that can be
expended each day on the tasks in
Block B. Starting from day one (1),
enter this number in the appropriate
column and continue through the
number of days required for the sum
of entries to equal that in Block C.
The second and succeeding tasks in a
sequence may not start from day one
(1). (Example - If engine removal
requires three (3) days and must be
done before engine supporting mounts
could be removed then this task would
start on day four (4)). (If more
than 12 flow days are involved use
additional forms).

         Note: For multi shift operations
                base this analysis on the
                number of shifts rather than
                days.

8. Block F   Enter the total of Block C.

9. Block G   Compute and enter the number of
work positions (round to the
nearest whole number) as
indicated, self-explanatory.

         NOTE: The flow/cycle time shall be
                rounded to the highest number
                in Block E having an entry.

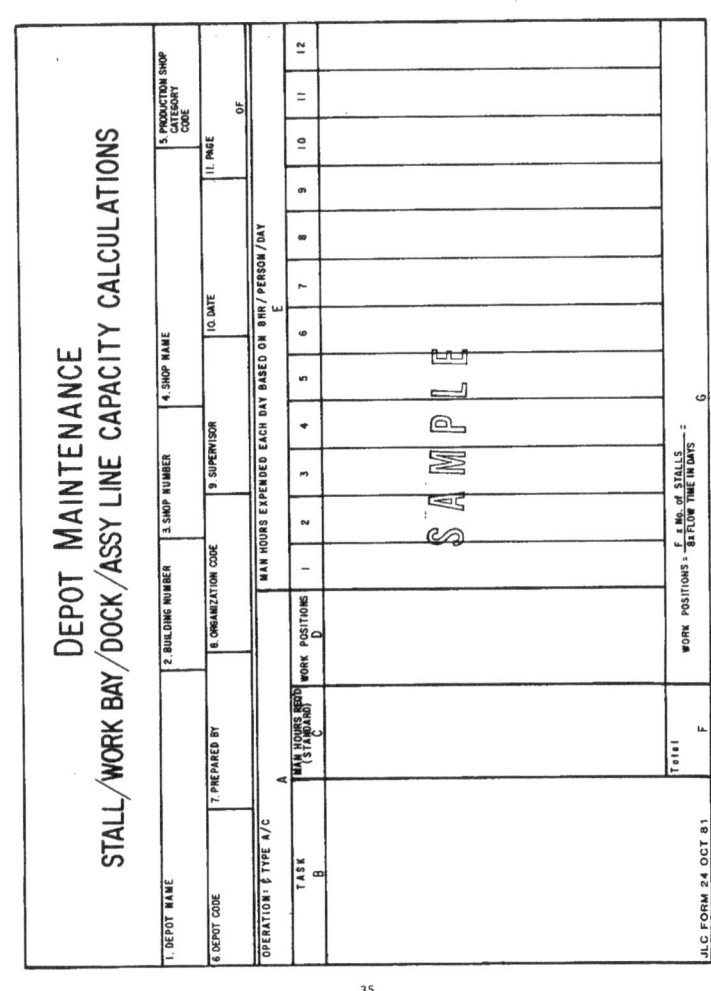

DEPOT MAINTENANCE
STALL/WORK BAY/DOCK/ASSY LINE CAPACITY CALCULATIONS

| 1. DEPOT NAME | | 2. BUILDING NUMBER | 3. SHOP NUMBER | 4. SHOP NAME | 5. PRODUCTION SHOP CATEGORY CODE |
| 6. DEPOT CODE | 7. PREPARED BY | 8. ORGANIZATION CODE | 9. SUPERVISOR | 10. DATE | 11. PAGE   OF |

MAN HOURS EXPENDED EACH DAY BASED ON 8HR / PERSON / DAY

OPERATION: & TYPE A/C													
TASK B	MAN HOURS REQ'D (STANDARD) C	WORK POSITIONS D	1	2	3	4	5	6	7	8	9	10	11	12

S A M P L E

Total | F |

WORK POSITIONS = $\dfrac{F \times No.\ of\ STALLS}{8 \times FLOW\ TIME\ IN\ DAYS}$ = G

JLC FORM 24 OCT 81

35

CAPACITY CALCULATIONS

INSTRUCTIONS FOR PREPARATION
OF JLC FORM 25
"REPORTING OF UNUTILIZED SPACE"

1. General

Unutilized space in the custody of the maintenance activity
represents potential capacity. This potential capacity shall
be reported separately on JLC Form 25. Only the physical
capacity will be reported. Peacetime Capacity, if required,
will be computed by JADMAG through application of an averaged
direct labor factor.

2. Blocks 1 through 13:   Complete these as required - self
                            explanatory.

                            NOTE: (1) Block 8 - a drawing may
                                   not exist and the capacity
                                   estimated. If so, leave
                                   blank.

                                   (2) Block 12. Use an
                                   availability factor of 95.

36

Unutilized Space

1.-DEPOT NAME	2. PREPARED BY	3. PHONE NUMBER	4. DATE
5. DEPOT CODE	6. BUILDING NO.	7. ASSIGNED P.S.C. AND F.A.C. CODE	
8. DRAWING NUMBER	9. TOTAL SHOP AREA	10. WORK POSITIONS	
11. GROSS CAPACITY	12. AVAILABILITY FACTOR (.95)	13. POTENTIAL PHYSICAL CAPACITY	

NOTE: (1) PEACETIME CAPACITY NOT REPORTED FOR UNUTILIZED SPACE

Remarks:

SAMPLE

JLC FORM 25 OCT 81

INSTRUCTIONS FOR PREPARATION
OF JLC FORM 26
"REPORTING OF GENERAL SHOP SUPPORT - PSC 110"

1. General

Only those assigned indirect functions shall be reported on JLC
Form 26. Total visibility of all assigned aeronautical depot
maintenance space is required by JADMAG to properly conduct
required analysis and to ensure inclusion of all space.

2. General Shop Support falls into three categories:

110A. That covered indirect area which provides support solely
to that specific production shop category code. These areas
will be coded as 110A plus a numeric code for the applicable
production Shop Category of the shop, e.g., 110A 103. This
coding includes technical file centers, toolcribs, production
centers, washrooms, lunch areas, dressing areas, locker rooms,
production supervisory and clerical support office areas,
restrooms, multi-purpose/main aisles, stairwells, auxilliary
equipment rooms walls, etc.

110B. That covered area which provides support to two or more
Production Shop Category codes. The proration of support space
should be based on the percentage of the total building space
occupied by a specific shop category. This category will
include the space required to directly support or service a
production area as follows:

   a. External boundary aisles and lanes.

   b. Lunch, rest, smoking and shower room.

   c. Utility areas within the building.

   d. Maintenance inventory control centers.

   e. Direct support office areas. This is space occupied
by an organization whose primary function is to provide
supervision, planning, scheduling, and controlling of the
production operation. These personnel act as intermediaries
between the directorate of administration and shop production
functions to accomplish the direct physical aspects of
logistical support. The following will be included:

      (1) Planners, schedulers, and material expediters.

      (2) Quality inspectors.

(3) Engineering technicians.

(4) Section supervisors and clerical personnel when these offices are part of the above areas.

    f. Receiving and dispatch areas.

    g. Temporary storage areas.

Areas in this category will be coded 110B plus an appropriate numeric code for that portion attributable to PSC 101 through 109.

110C. Those covered indirect spaces which provide general support to all depot maintenance operation. These include functions such as management, administration, engineering, clerical offices, cafeterias, plant maintenance, central or general storage, quality assurance facilities, and any area provided to non-maintenance activities, such as personnel offices, credit union offices, dispensaries, etc.

3. Instructions for form completion:

    A. Items 1 through 7 - Self explanatory.

    B. Item A - Enter identification code outlined in paragraph 2 above.

    C. Item B - Enter brief description of space use, e.g., washroom, cafeteria, locker room, etc.

    D. Item C - Enter brief description of the specific function supported by 110A or 110B.

    E. Item D - Enter the area in square feet of the space itemized in Item C.

GENERAL DEPOT SUPPORT

1.-DEPOT NAME						2.-BLDG. NUMBER	
3.-PREPARED BY		4.-ORGANIZATION CODE			5.-PHONE NUMBER	6.-DATE	7.-PAGE
8. CODE	A. CODE	B. FUNCTION		C. FUNCTION		D. AREA SUPPORTED	

SAMPLE

TOTAL

Remarks:

40 40 40

REFERENCES

1. DOD Instruction 4151.15, "Depot Maintenance Support Programming Policies", 22 November 1976

2. DOD Handbook 4151.15H, "Depot Maintenance Production Shop Capacity Measurement Handbook", 28 July 1976

3. DOD Handbook 7220.29H, "Department of Defense Depot Maintenance and Maintenance Support Cost Accounting and Production Reporting Handbook", 21 October 1975

4. DOD Instruction 4165.3 "DOD Facility Classes and Construction Categories", 1 September 1972

5. NAVFAC P-72 "Category Codes for Navy Facilities Assets".

6. AFLCR 66-4, (C5) Chapter 5, AFLC Maintenance Facility Master Plan System (G004K)

DISTRIBUTION

DEPARTMENT OF THE NAVY.   425

Ship bulk to: Defense Printing Service, Distribution Section,
               BD831, Pentagon, Washington, DC 20350

(For DPS)
Distribution: SNDL: FKA1 (15 copies each), A4A (25 copies)
Copy to: (2 cys ea) SNDL A3, C37A1, FJ89, FKM9, FKM13,
               FKM15, FKM15, FKM17, FKN1, FKP1, FKQ2, FKQ3,
               FKR1B, FKR5, FKR7E, FKP7

Stocked: CO, NAVPUBFORMCEN, 5801 Tabor Ave., Phila. PA 19120
          (100)

DEPARTMENT OF THE AIR FORCE: 1400

HQ AFLC   1200

     PDO 4000
     2750 ABW/DAPR
     Wright-Patterson AFB, OH 45433

HQ AFSC   200

     PDO 4015
     Andrews AFB, DC 20334

DEPARTMENT OF THE ARMY.   1200

HQ DARCOM/DRXAM-ABS   For stock only   200
5001 Eisenhower Ave, Alexandria, VA 22233

Letterkenny Army Depot.   1000
ATTN: SDSLE-SAAD, Chambersburg, PA 17201

US MARINE CORPS   100

Marine Corps Distribution

     6025   (5)
     7000 160 (2)
     7000 161 (3)
     7000 167 (1)
     7000 176 (4)
Copy to: 8145001

Commandant of the Marine Corps
(Code HOSP-2C) (45 copies)
Washington, DC 20380

Commanding General (55 copies)
Marine Corps Logistics Base
Albany, GA 31704

42

O. L. TALBOT
Assistant Deputy Chief of
Naval Material (Logistics)
Naval Material Command

WILLIAM R. CARROLL, Colonel,
USAF
Director of Administration

JAMES P. MULLINS, General,
USAF
Commander
Air Force Logistics Command

FREDERICK P. HALLSWORTH,
Lt Col, USAF
Director of Administration

ROBERT T. MARSH, General, USAF

Commander
Air Force Systems Command

JUDITH L. TILT, Maj, GS
Adjutant General

DONALD R. KEITH, General, USA
Commander
US Army Material Development
and Readiness Command

H. A. HATCH
Lieutenant General
US Marine Corps
Deputy Chief of Staff
Installations and Logistics

www.ingramcontent.com/pod-product-compliance
Lightning Source LLC
Chambersburg PA
CBHW080917290526
45795CB00007BA/2548